P9-DWI-890

Volume 6
Komi Can't Communicate
Tomohito Oda
ご利用の集積場 No.
燃やせるゴミ
毎週 月・木
プラスチック資源物
毎週 金
紙資源
毎週 水
燃やせないゴミ
危険物
粗大ごみ
2・4回目
火曜日

Komi Can't Communicate

Volume 6

Tomohito Oda

Contents 6

Komi Can't Communicate

Karaoke with a communication disorder—

Communication 73: After-Party

Good job, everyone! Our maid cafe at the culture festival was a huge success!!
EEP!
YAAAAAY

IS EVERYONE HERE?!
ROLL CALL!
ONE!
TWO!
THREE!
FOUR!
...!
UM, I'LL COUNT THE REST.

NOW LET'S GO SING KARA-OKE!!
KARAOKE
DASHDASHDASH
YAAAAAY
NAJIMI'S SO ENER-GETIC...

WE'RE GOING TO KARAOKE FOR THE AFTER-PARTY. IS THAT OKAY?
!

"Yes."
!

"I've always wanted to do karaoke in a group."
OH, REALLY?
CAN KOMI SING?

WELL, LET'S GO THEN!
NOD

FIDGET FIDGET
...!

UM ...
... SHOULD WE RUN TOO?
!

...
...

KARAOKE
KARAOKE
Now let's go sing karaoke!!

!
GLANCE
!
GLANCE
IS THIS YOUR FIRST TIME?

!
"I came with my family once."
HUH?
AND ...
...DID YOU SING?

"Only my mother sang."
...
OH...
LOW-KEY

DIVIDE UP INTO THREE ROOMS!
TUMP
11
Tadano and Komi's room
12
TUMP

WE'VE GOT THREE ROOMS!
TUMP
11
Tadano and Komi's room
12

UM...
SMUSH
Tadano and Komi's room
12

?!
11
Tadano and Komi's room
12
SMUSHHHH

11
12
They agreed to take turns.

LET'S ORDER DRINKS! CALL OUT YOUR ORDER!
OKAAAAY

COLA!
MAKE THAT TWO COLAS!
GINGER ALE!
HOT LEMON TEA!
MELON SODA!
I'LL HAVE OOLONG TEA!
OOH, ME TOO!
CORN SOUP!
CAFÉ AU LAIT!
...

Um, that'll be 12 colas! Thanks!
SERI-OUSLY?!

PUNCH IN YOUR SONGS, GUYS!
!

Nervous about singing
TREMMMBLE
UM, YOU DON'T HAVE TO FORCE YOURSELF.

YES, YOU DO!
SWIK
GLEAM
EVERYONE HAS TO SING AT LEAST ONE SONG!
GLEAM
URGH

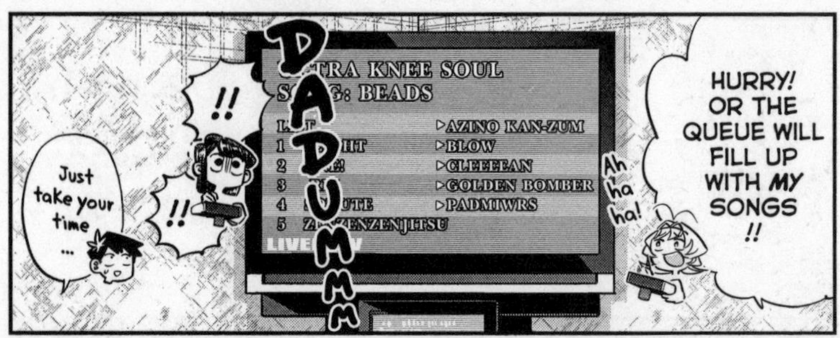
HURRY! OR THE QUEUE WILL FILL UP WITH MY SONGS !!
Ah ha ha!
TRA KNEE SOUL
G: BEADS
AZINO KAN-ZUM
BLOW
CLEEEEAN
GOLDEN BOMBER
PADMIWRS
DADUMMM
!!
!!
Just take your time ...

...
...
Every-thing is but a dreeeam!

Not sure about the song she chose
...
Laugh and let the light shine!

UL-TRAAA! KNEEEEE !!
YAAAH !!
JOLT
YAAAY
?!
SENT

Are you havin' fun yet ?!
BWAAAAH
Well, I've got another song for ya!
That's enough, Najimi!!
Take a seat !!
AH HA HA HA HA

Komi input her song selection, but now she's nervous about singing in front of everyone.
SHA SHAKA
SHA SHA SHAKA
SHA KA

I'M NEXT! PREPARE TO AWARD ME A HIGH SCORE!

We Never Ever Meet
Miki Kitano
We never ever meeeeet!
I SING THIS FOR KOMI!
HEAR MY PASSION, KOMI!!
Ohhh, how I tremble!
Say you looove me! Even if it's a lieee!

BAM
98 PTS
YEEEEAH
YES! I ROCK!!

Increasingly nervous as her turn approaches
TREMMMMBLE
MY SINGING TOUCHED HER AND MADE HER TREMBLE!!

I'M NEXT...
MWA HA HA...
THE TIME IS AT HAND!

Endless World's End
From Lost Endless World
HEH HEH HEH... I AM THE SINGER SUPREME !!
It's Lost world! It's Lost world! If you can do it do it!!
IN EXPECTATION OF THIS DAY (DOING KARAOKE WITH EVERYONE), I MEMORIZED "ENDLESS WORLD'S END," THE THEME SONG FOR THE HIT ANIME LOST ENDLESS WORLD, RIGHT DOWN TO THE SNIPPETS OF DIALOGUE!!
MY ATTENTION TO DETAIL WILL STUN THEM!!
*Snippets: "We will not suffer destruction!!

TADUMMM
CLAP CLAP
Do I know this?
CLAP CLAP
Is it from an anime?
HMM. I WAS HOPING FOR MORE ...

Incredibly nervous
TRMBL
TREMBLE
TRMBL
TRMBL
TREMMMBLE
AHH! BUT IT RESONATED WITH MY ALLY!! SHE GOT GOOSE BUMPS!
PHEW

Spring and Autumn Amigos
Haruo and Akira
Sing it! We two are...
...one together! Yeah!
KYAAAAH♡
TREMMMBLE
Bear o' the Forest
Foreign nursery rhyme
One d-d-day in th-th-th...
...th-the f-f-f-forest...
Huh? Is this techno?
Cool!
TREMMMBLE
367 Days
NY
I will forever remember...
...your eyes and haaair...
Off by a beat
Off by two beats
SHE'S WAY OFF!
HUFF
HUFF
Be My Shrine Maiden
From Love ☆ Star
Ignorant 13 Kilometers!
I'll kiss you--yeah!--in your shrine-maiden outfit!
Is it soft?
HE'S GOT A GOOD VOICE!!
JUDDDERRR

TRA LA LA LA LA
And then it was Komi's turn.
WOOHOO
Yaaaaay! Komiiiiii!!

Synthetic Fiber Handkerchief
Yumi Ota
...
...

!!
Missed the moment to start singing
...!
...!!
OH NO ...

...!!
...?!
!!!
I CAN HEAR HER!
LOUD AND CLEAR!
IT'S ONLY AUDIBLE TO THE PURE OF HEART!
Auditory halluci-nation
?!

GLOOM
Almost crying
CLAP
CLAP
YAAAAAAY
CLAP

Fixed Point Observation
OH, I'M NEXT...

With my zoom lens I seeeee...
...the unseeeeen!
!

IGNORE
N-NO ONE IS LISTENING !!
IGNORE

HOW SAD...
I DIDN'T REALLY WANT THEM TO...
...BUT STILL!
IT'S STILL SAD!

SHAKA
SHAKA

SHAKA
SHAKA
...!
in darkness
race down the street
and my past
still binds me

Communication 73 — The End

FIXED POINT OBSERVATION
BY BEEF OR CHICKEN

AT 3 P.M. I FIX A CAMERA ON THE ROOF
WITH A SWEET CANDY IN MY POCKET

FIVE HOURS LATER HE APPEARS WITH A BAG
THE SEARCH FOR THE CRIMINAL BEGINS

I WAS WISE TO DRINK BEFORE DARK
BECAUSE MY HANDS STOPPED SHAKING

WITH MY ZOOM LENS I SEE THE UNSEEN
I GET ROWDY SEVERAL OF THAT ARE BORN
THAT, THAT, WHAT IS THAT? WORDS FAIL ME
AT THE MYSTERIOUS WORD WE PONDERED
(OH, YEAH! UH-HUH!)

CONTINUED IN PART 2

Komi Can't Communicate

Komi Can't Communicate

...
BRRRRR
Looking for some-thing warm to wear

Looking for some-thing warm to wear
BRRRRR
...

Look-ing for...
...
BRRRRRRR
BRRRRRRR
...
... some-thing warm ...

BRRRRRR
...but she doesn't have any-thing!!

Komi Can't Communicate
Communication 74: Shopping with Dad

FRIZZ
PWUF
PWUF
PWOINK
PWOINK
GLOWRRRRR
Doesn't like it

GOOD MORNING, SHOKO.

...
Wants to go clothes shopping
...
Wants to go clothes shopping

HERE. HAM 'N' EGG SANDWICHES. AND EAT YOUR SALAD!
...
...

...
Can't say it
...

SHOKO, YOU SHOULD GO CLOTHES SHOPPING WITH YOUR FATHER TODAY!
!!
HELP HIM PICK OUT AN OUTFIT!

...
...

...
TWITCH
JOLT
...!

HMPH!
PHEW
For new clothes? She'll do it!

Indicating she can shop for herself first
SWIP
...!

Indicating he'll wait right here
SWUP
!
Too embar-rassed to go into a girls' clothing store

WANDER
WANDER
WANDER

Still can't go into clothing stores alone
?

werenot
?!

Clothes from junior high
She thinks they're dorky and don't fit her right.
SHUDDER

Shop-ping with dad
She doesn't want to be seen.
SHUDDER

!!
!!
?
?
GOCHISOU

CHIPS
CHIPS
TADAAAH
...
...
?!!

GLOOOOM
!

Can quickly choose clothes for other people
SHWUF
SHWIF
Emotional about his daughter helping him
BLOOP
Has the world's best daughter
?!

WHOA
Thinks he'll buy it
...
...
Or maybe not?
...
SHF
...
BO OM
Thank you, sir!
Credit card

Wants him to try this on
HMF!
HMF!

HM?
KOMI?
JOLLLLLT
?!

?!
?!
MY SISTER AND I ARE GETTING AN ANNIVERSARY PRESENT FOR OUR PARENTS.
WHAT'S WRONG? WHY DO YOU SEEM SO...

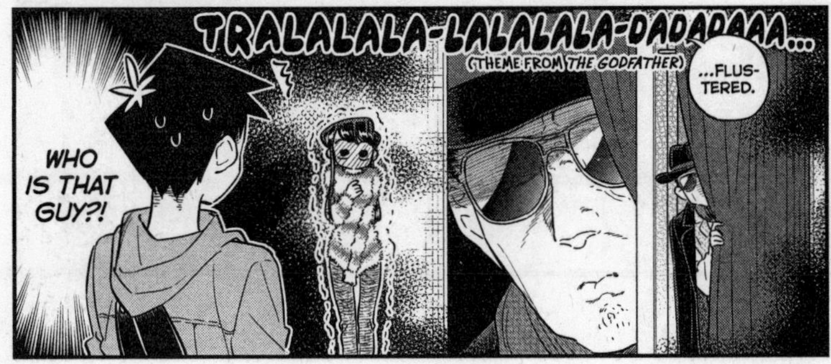
TRALALALA-LALALALA-DADADAAA...
(THEME FROM THE GODFATHER)
...FLUS-TERED.
WHO IS THAT GUY?!

RMMMM
...
MMBL
ARE YOU KOMI'S DAD?
N-nice to meet you...
HE'S SCARY !!
KOMI'S DAD IS SCARY!!
TRALALALA-LALALALA-DADADAAA...
(THEME FROM THE GODFATHER)
UM, WHAT DO YOU DO FOR A LI–
ULP! MAYBE I BETTER NOT ASK!!
TRALALALA-LALALALA-DADADAAA...
(THE GODFATHER)
UH, SORRY FOR BOTHERING YOU.
I'LL GO NOW, SO...
!
GLOOM

mars
wild store
dance&economy
Welcome!
Still can't go in
TREMBLE
TREMBLE
KOMIIII!

!
HI! I HAVEN'T SEEN YOU IN A WHILE!
!!

?
I THOUGHT IT MIGHT BE EASIER FOR YOU TO GO IN WITH ANOTHER GIRL...
...SO I BROUGHT MY SISTER.
!!!
TRALALALA...
(GODFATHER)
...

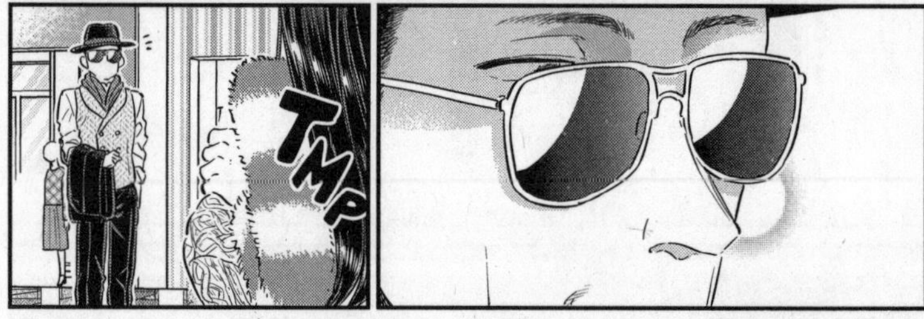

Communication 74 — The End

He gets an allowance...

...and often dips into next month's too.

But he's...

...satisfied.

Komi Can't Communicate

Komi Can't Communicate

Communication 75: Fantasies, Part 1

Who would you date? —Najimi—
AH HA HA HA
SOMETHING IS HAPPENING!

WE WENT ON A LOT OF RIDES!
YEAH, I'M EXHAUST-ED!
ALPAKA

OKAY! LET'S TAKE A BREAK!
FLAGO

Oops! Watch out!
LICK
HUH?!

Tee hee!

It's your fault! You should be more care-ful!

LET'S RIDE AN-OTHER RIDE!
HUH?! MORE ?!
NICE! YOU'RE LIKE FRIENDS!
THE ICE CREAM ON NAJIMI'S NOSE WAS A NICE TOUCH!
THIS IS HOW THEY'RE GOING TO DECIDE ?!

*This scene was pure fantasy. Any relation to real persons or events is coincidental.

Who would you date? –Agari–
THEY'RE IMAGINING SOMETHING AGAIN!
SHE'S LATE...
S-SORRY!
I H-HAD TROUBLE PICKING AN OUTFIT!
BYOINNNG
W-WERE YOU WAITING LONG?!
NO, UM... I JUST GOT HERE! ♪
OH, TH-THAT'S GOOD.
THAT'S QUITE A BOLD DRESS.
Y-YEAH, I'M...

...AL-LOWING IT...
...JUST FOR YOU.

Who would you date? —Yamai—

POUT

I KNOW DINNER WASN'T GOOD...
...BUT PLEASE DON'T SULK.
QUIET! IT'S YOUR FAULT FOR HAVING SUCH POOR TASTE!

I'M SORRY.
HERE, THIS IS FOR YOU.
IT'S A PRESENT TO CELE-BRATE...
...OUR ONE-MONTH ANNIVER-SARY.

W-WHAT?! THESE AREN'T CUTE AT ALL!

YOU REALLY DO HAVE POOR TASTE!

Who would you date? —Naka-naka—
AGH!
URGH!

OOF!
GAH!
UNGH ...

?
NO, NOT THAT WAY.
HERE. LET ME DO IT.
GO THE OTHER WAY. THERE'S A TREASURE CHEST OVER THERE.
!

TAK TAK TAK TAK
CHACHING
WOW! You got it!

YOU BET I DID!

BLACK

*This scene is pure fantasy. Any relation to real persons or events is coincidental.

Who would you date? -Inaka-

MY NAME IS SHINO-BINO.
SKREEEE
I SERVE MY MASTER IN THIS RURAL AREA.
A MONO-LOGUE ?!
T

Hallooo!
!
THE HARVEST LOOKS MIGHTY TASTY!
THIS IS INAKA.
SHE LIVES IN THE HOUSE NEXT TO MY MASTER'S.

SHINO-BINO! HERE! TRY ONE!
ALL RIGHT. JUST ONE.
THANK YOU.
CHOMP

DON'T IT TASTE WONDER-FUL?

Who would you date?
—Makeru—

BRR! IT'S COLD!
LET'S GO HOME FOR A HOT DRINK.
YEAH, GOOD IDEA.

RACE YOU THERE !!
WHOOOSH
HEY, NO FAIR!

YAY!

I WIN!

HUH?
WHAT THE?
THAT'S PER-FECT!
OH, RIGHT. YOU *LIKE* MAKERU.
CAN YADANO ACTUALLY BE CUTE?!
*This scene is pure fantasy. Any relation to real persons or events is coincidental.

Who would you date? —Komi—

AND NOW WE COME TO *KOMI*...
CAN WE DO THIS?
IT'S GOTTA BE A GOOD STORY!
IS *THAT* WHAT THIS IS ABOUT ?!

Five minutes later
HM? HA HA...
I GOT NOTHING.
I'M DRAWING A BLANK.

Ten minutes later
GRAAARRRGH!
I SIMPLY CAN'T IMAGINE US ALONE TOGETHER!!!
IT'S BEYOND MY ABILITY !!
?!

Who would you date? -Komi-

THANK YOU FOR THE MEAL.
IT WAS WON-DERFUL.
!
NOD

I'LL WASH THE DISHES.
!
SHAKE SHAKE

ROCK-PAPER-SCISSORS FOR IT?
ONE...
TWO...
!
!

SPSHHH
SLOSH
SLOSH

!
SPSHHH
SLOSH
SLOSH
REALLY, YOU DON'T HAVE TO.
BUT THANK YOU.

BMP

Communication 75 — The End

The Boys' Fantasy Ranking

#1—Nakanaka!!

Komi Can't Communicate

Komi Can't Communicate

Komi Can't

Communication 76: Delinquent

THAT WAS NERVE-WRACKING!

BUT ALL I DID WAS ASK ABOUT MY CLASS!!
BABMP
BABMP

I CAUGHT A COLD RIGHT WHEN SCHOOL STARTED AND ENDED UP STAYING HOME IN BED FOR A WEEK.
MOAN
GROAN
AFTER THAT, I HAD DIFFICULTY TAKING THE PLUNGE.
Stopped at the gate
I'LL GO TOMORROW.
YEAH, TOMORROW.
TOMORROW, I DEFINITELY ...

BEFORE I KNEW IT, THE SEASON HAD CHANGED!
BAM
Winter

I CHANGED OVER SUMMER VACATION. I WORKED OUT TO IMPROVE MYSELF...
FIVE HUN-DRED MORE!!
...AND DYED MY HAIR TO AVOID GETTING BULLIED!

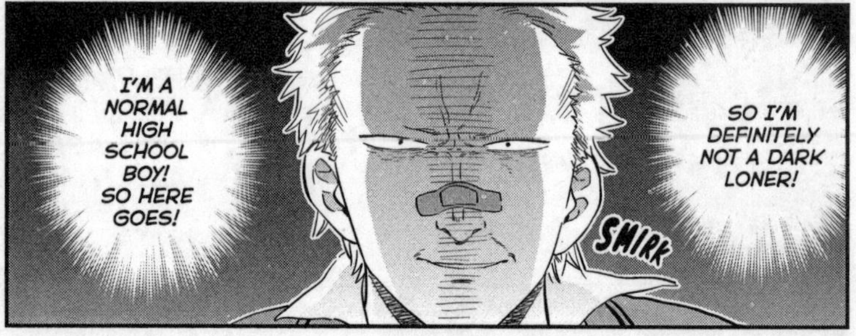
SO I'M DEFINITELY NOT A DARK LONER!
SMIRK
I'M A NORMAL HIGH SCHOOL BOY! SO HERE GOES!

...
...

AW, MAN! I'M SO NER-VOUS!
Who's that thug?!!
FREEEEZE
He's just standing there!
Scary...

RATTLE

FL INCH
BAM
Bumped the door with his knee

What's his problem?
Who is that?
He kicked the door...
Now it hurts

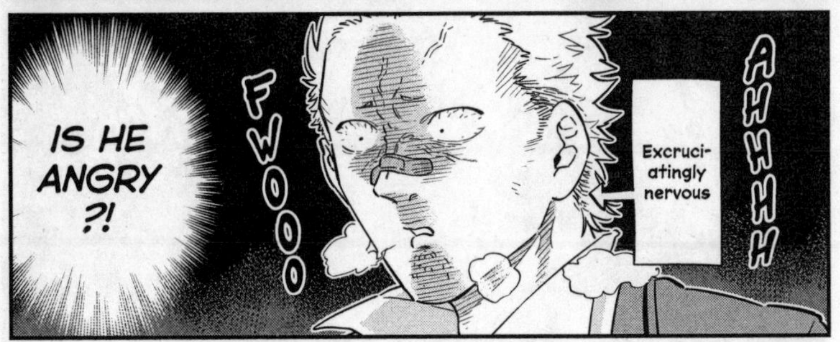
AHHHHH
Excruci-atingly nervous
FWOOOO
IS HE ANGRY ?!

SHUF

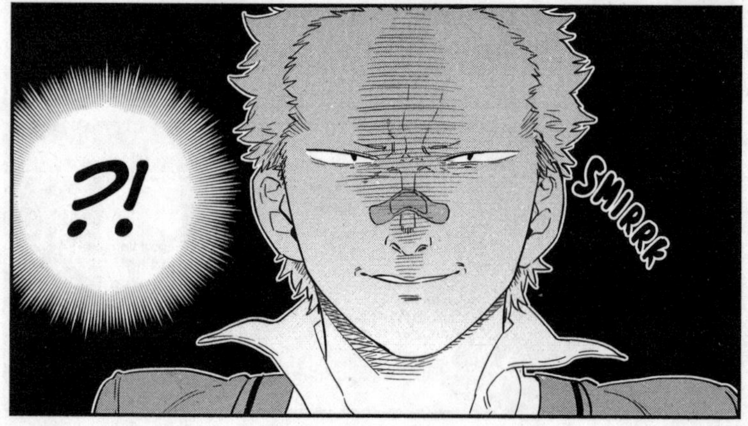
?!
SMIRRK

AGH! I DON'T KNOW WHERE I SIT!
Expla-nation for that →
I'LL ATTRACT ATTENTION IF I GO UP FRONT, SO I'LL STAND IN BACK ...

...AND WAIT FOR THE TEACHER.
SHUF
ULP... EVERY-ONE'S STARING AT ME!

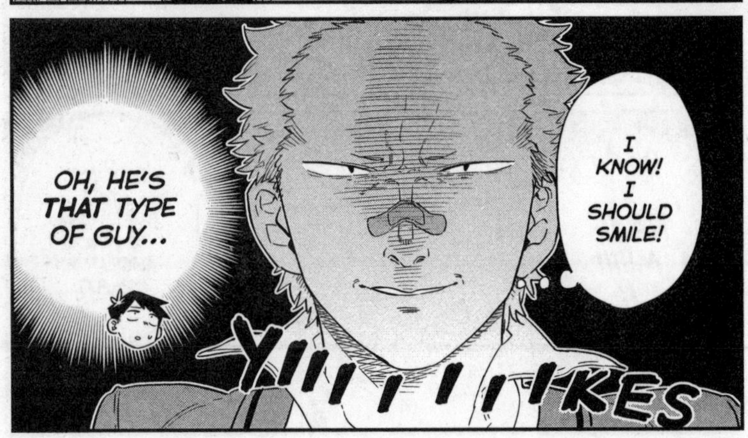
I KNOW! I SHOULD SMILE!
OH, HE'S THAT TYPE OF GUY...
YIIIIIIIKES

SMIIIRK
W-what's his deal?
I bet he's up to no good!!
Someone talk to him!!

Good morning!
Oh! Katai?!
NAJIMI! OUR SAVIOR!!
*Najimi is old friends with everyone.

What's up?! I haven't seen you in forever!
Ha ha! You've really changed!

DRRRAG
I DON'T WANT EVERYONE TO KNOW ABOUT MY PAST!
I SHOULD EXPLAIN THAT TO NAJIMI!!
NAJI-MIIIII!!

OOPS... FORGOT TO SMILE!
SMIIIIRK
H-HE GOT RID OF NAJIMIII !!
Najimi went to the rest-room.

FIDGET FIDGET
BDUMP BDUMP
ISN'T ANYONE GOING TO TALK TO ME?
IF WE TALK TO HIM, HE'LL KILL US!!
FIDGET FIDGET
BDUMP BDUMP

LET'S SOOTHE OUR-SELVES BY LOOKING AT KOMI!
GAAAAAAAAAAAZE
GLOMP GLOMP
?!

WHY DID EVERYONE GATHER OVER THERE?
YAY
I WONDER WHAT'S UP.
IS SOMEONE POPULAR OVER THERE?
YAY

MUTTER
Should I go see?
MUTTER
MUTTER
...if I do...
MUTTER
But...
MUTTER
HE'S MUTTERING TO HIMSELF... IT'S HORRIFYING!!

I NEED TO CHANGE! SO I'LL JUST MARCH RIGHT OVER!
SMILE, SMILE ...
SMIIIIRK
YIKES! HE'S COMING THIS WAY!!

WE MUST PROTECT KOMI FROM HARM!
DOOOOM
TH- THE CLASS DELIN-QUENTS !!

BUMP

D(O YOU MIND) ...
D...
...(IF) I...
I DIDN'T SPEAK CLEARLY! DID THEY UNDER-STAND?
D...I... DIE?!!

SWIP
THEY DIDN'T SAY ANYTHING, SO I THINK THEY UNDERSTOOD.
PHEW
You boys are useless!
Are you really delinquents?!

WHAT WAS EVERYONE STARING...

...AT?

SH...

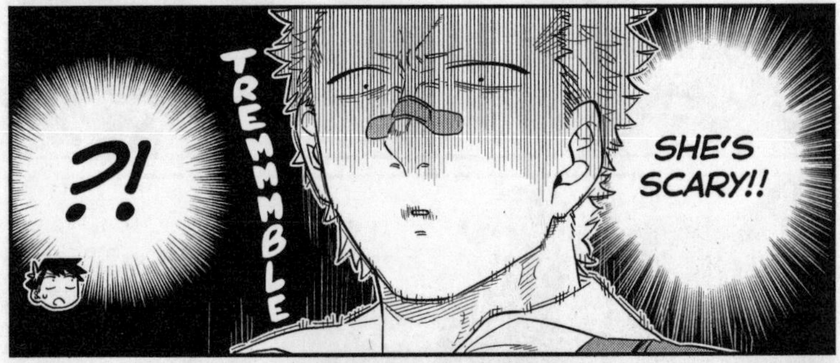
SHE'S SCARY!!
TREMMMBLE
?!

SHE HAS THE MOST INTIMIDATING AURA I'VE EVER SEEN!!
SHE'S LOOKING AT ME... NO, SHE'S GLARING!! BUT WHY?! I CAN'T HANDLE IT!!

I NEED TO SIT DOWN...
FUMP
JITTER JITTER JITTER JITTER
?!
HE SAT DOWN ?!

TAKE A DEEP BREATH ...
WHE-E-E-E-W...
?!

GLANCE

SHE'S STILL STARING AT ME!
Too scared to move
PEOPLE USUALLY LOOK AWAY FROM ME!

BUT...
...THIS MIGHT BE THE FIRST TIME...
...I'VE EVER MADE EYE CONTACT!

OH, RIGHT!
REMEMBER CHAPTER 4, PAGE 116, OF CONVERSATION TECHNIQUES EVEN MONKEYS CAN HANDLE !!
Conversation Techniques Even Monkeys Can Have Conversations
"AID COMMUNICATION BY MAKING EYE CONTACT"!!

KASHUDDERRRRRRR
THAT'S WHY SHE'S STARING AT ME!!
SH-SHE WANTS TO HAVE A CONVERSATION!
G-GOOD! SO DO I!

STAAAAAAAAARE
It's a stare down...
Petrified
Petrified
Is he picking a fight?!

UM...
...YOUR NAME IS KATAI, RIGHT?
!

Huh?
DARN IT! MY VOICE HAS GOTTEN REALLY LOW SINCE IT CHANGED! UNLESS I TRY TO MAKE IT HIGHER, I SOUND ANGRY!!

HE PROB-ABLY THINKS I'M A JERK...

YOU MISSED A LOT OF SCHOOL.

SHALL I SHOW YOU AROUND?

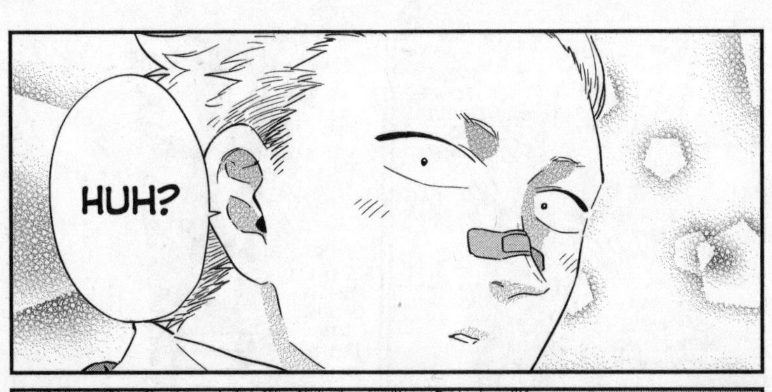
HUH?

YEAH...
...I'D LIKE THAT.

?!

Communication 76 — The End

Communication Power
Beauty
Scariness
Knowledge
Strength
COMMUNICATION MASTER

Komi Can't
Communicate

Komi Can't Communicate

Communication 77: Fantasies, Part 2

Who would you date? —One-mine—
FWSH
FWSH

ISN'T THE WEATHER BEAUTIFUL TODAY?
YES, IT REALLY IS!
FWUP

CHECK IT OUT!
I MADE US LUNCH!
TADA
WHOA!

SWIK

CHMP

AND THEN SILENCE! SHE JUST GAZES AT ME ...
Sublime!
SHE'S SO BISTERLY!*
*Big sisterly
SHE HAS A VERY REASSURING VIBE!
*This scene is pure fantasy. Any relation to real persons or events is coincidental.

Who would you date? -Otori-

I'M HOME ...
WELCOME BAAAACK!
WOULD YOU LIKE DIIINNER?
TMP
TMP

...
WHAT'S WROOONG ?

SWUF
...
WORK ...
I MESSED UP BIG-TIME.
UGH ...
I MIGHT GET FIRED.

THERE, THERE... IT'S OKAY.

IT'LL ALL WORK OOOOUT!

Who would you date? —Komi—
MUTTER
MUTTER
HM? A HISTORICAL SETTING ?!
T

THIS PLAN WILL LEAD TO THE ULTIMATE DEMISE...
...OF THE SHOGUNATE.
ONLY THEN SHALL THE SUN RISE...
...TO SHINE UPON JAPAN'S FUTURE.
INDEED.
WELL THIS IS LIGHTHEARTED !!
T

YOU ARE ALL UNDER ARREST !!
BABAAAAM
WHO IS THAT MAN ?!!

Yah!
SILENCE!!
THOK
A PINWHEEL ?!

I AM YOUR OPPO-NENT!

PREPARE TO LOSE YOUR HEADS!

Communication 77 — The End

Komi Can't Communicate

Komi Can't Communicate

WHSH

Communication 78: Winter Arrives

AHHH
FWOOO
ST
AAAAAAAARE
CRINGE

TMP
CHILL
JOLT

?!
?!

?
BABMP BABMP BABMP BABMP BABMP BABMP
JOLLLLT

JOLT
CHILL

Communication 78 — The End

Communication 79: Studying at Nakanaka's House

It's winter !!
Snowman pose!!
I'LL REFRAIN FROM COMMENT ...

BUT I THOUGHT YOU HATED WINTER.
I hate the cold!
But there are many great things about winter!
Christmas! New Year's! Electric blankets! The Hakone relay race!

And final exams.
Exams... You just had to go and mention that!
Curse you!!

Here's an idea! Let's study at Naka-naka's house !!
PWAAAAAAH
?!
NAJIMI JUST WANTS TO PLAY VIDEO GAMES !!

Naka-naka's house

YOU ARE ALL WELCOME AT MY CASTLE...
...EXCEPT FOR HER.

EXCEPT FOR WHO?
WHO DOES SHE MEAN, KOMI?
YOU! I MEAN YOU!

HUH? WHY? AREN'T WE FRIENDS?
YOU CAN'T INVITE KOMI TO YOUR HOUSE BUT NOT ME!!
FRIENDS? I DON'T THINK SO.
YOU'RE JUST JEALOUS, YOU HUSSY!
UH-OH! THOSE TWO ALWAYS CLASH!

We're com-ing in!
1
2
Good night!
FWIP
NAJIMI WENT TO SLEEP?!
In someone else's bed?!
TAKEHU

KOMI! SIT BESIDE ME!
I NEED HELP WITH PHYSICS FORMU-LAS!
NO, SIT OVER HERE!
THE CUSHION OVER THERE SUCKS!
Why did Najimi come here?

HUH?
HOSTILITIES COMMENCED IN THE WAR FOR KOMI'S AFFECTION!
HUH?!

OH, RIGHT! KOMI, LET'S PLAY VIDEO GAMES!!
I BOUGHT SOME NEW ONES! AND THEY'RE EASY!
BUT WE CAME HERE TO STUDY...
NAKANAKA'S ATTACK: I DID IT FOR YOU, KOMI!

HUH? I DOUBT KOMI PLAYS VIDEO GAMES!!
SCOFF
VIDEO GAMES ARE FOR BOYS!
WHAT ?!
...
BUT YAMAI DODGES...

GIRLS TALK ABOUT LOVE!
Komi! Who do you like?
I like you! ♥
YAMAI'S ATTACK: BASICALLY CONFESSING HER LOVE!

...
UM... LET'S STUDY!
BUT IT HAS LITTLE EFFECT.

They began studying.
THE MOMENT I STEPPED INTO THIS ROOM...

...I NOTICED THAT EVERYTHING IS BLACK AND THAT THERE ARE LOTS OF ANIME AND MOVIE POSTERS...
There aren't any flowers!
...LIKE IT'S A NERDY BOY'S ROOM!
GAH!!
YAMAI DOES DAMAGE!

TH-THEN WHAT *SHOULD* A GIRL'S ROOM BE LIKE?
THAT'S EASY!

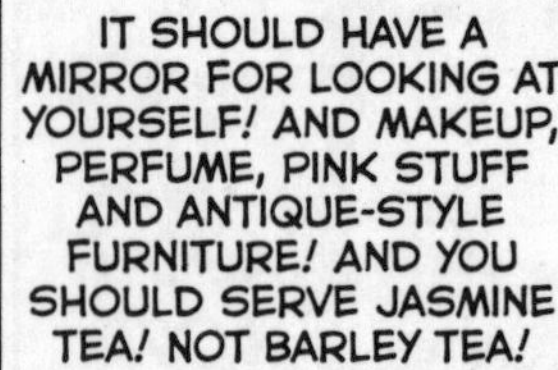
IT SHOULD HAVE A MIRROR FOR LOOKING AT YOURSELF! AND MAKEUP, PERFUME, PINK STUFF AND ANTIQUE-STYLE FURNITURE! AND YOU SHOULD SERVE JASMINE TEA! NOT BARLEY TEA!

NORMIE GIRL STUFF?
HUH?
NAKANAKA DOES DAMAGE!

I DON'T NEED ADVICE FROM A GIRL WHO DOESN'T HAVE PRETTY FINGERNAILS!

OH? BUT YOUR HAIR IS IN HORRENDOUS CONDITION!
IT'S BECAUSE YOU BLEACH IT!

YOU LIVE AT HOME, SO I BET YOU CAN'T COOK!
YOU LACK FEMI-NINITY!

FEMI-NINITY? (LOL)
YOU CAN'T PUT A NUMBER ON THAT, SO DON'T BOTHER COMPARING.
GIRLS ARE FRIGHTEN-ING...

MY FORTUNE SAID I'M MORE COMPATIBLE WITH KOMI!
Y
IS IT BECAUSE YOUR WHOLE LIFE IS ONLINE ?!
Y
YOU TALK LIKE AN OLD LADY! (LOL)
N
OH MY! MORE NORMIE GIRL STUFF! BUT FORTUNES ARE NON-SENSE!
N
ANYWAY! WHY DO YOU TALK WEIRD?!
Y
HOW OLD ARE YOU AGAIN ?
N
POOR KOMI!
T
SCRIBBLE SCRIBBLE SCRIBBLE SCRIBBLE SCRIBBLE

You're both important friends.

BLUSH
BLUSH
Silent bliss over Komi saying they're important friends

B-BUT WHAT IF YOU REALLY HAD TO CHOOSE?!
...

HOW ABOUT COMPETING VIA EXAM SCORES?
YOU SHUT YOUR FACE HOLE.
Y N
THEY AGREE ON SOMETHING!

I DON'T WANT KOMI TO HEAR THIS.
IF I'M PUSHY, SHE'LL HATE ME.
ARE YOU EVER NOT PUSHY?!

TH...
THERE MUST BE SOME WAY TO SETTLE THIS!
...

VIDEO GAMES!
...!

THAT'S IT! FIGHT'S ON!!
I'll join you!
THIS ALWAYS HAP-PENS!

A Fish in Troubled Waters

Communication 79 — The End

They also competed via exams.

	Japanese	Math	Science	Sociology	English	Total
Yamai	81	82	80	94	90	427
Nakanaka	81	96	99	75	76	427

Komi Can't Communicate

Komi Can't Communicate

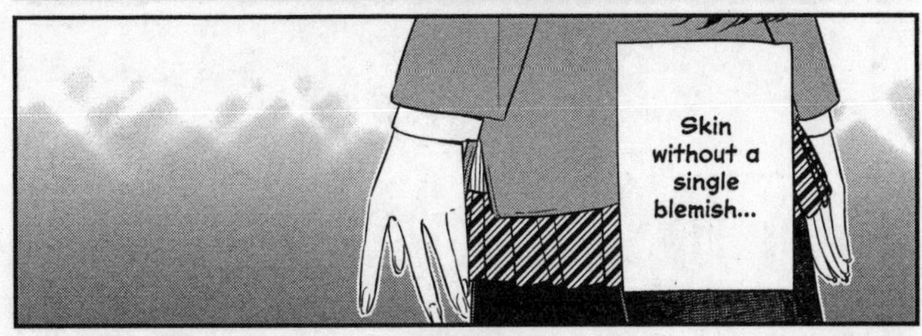

Luxurious dark black hair...

Skin without a single blemish...

Like a queen or mother goddess ...
...her presence is over-whelming.

She is **Komi.**

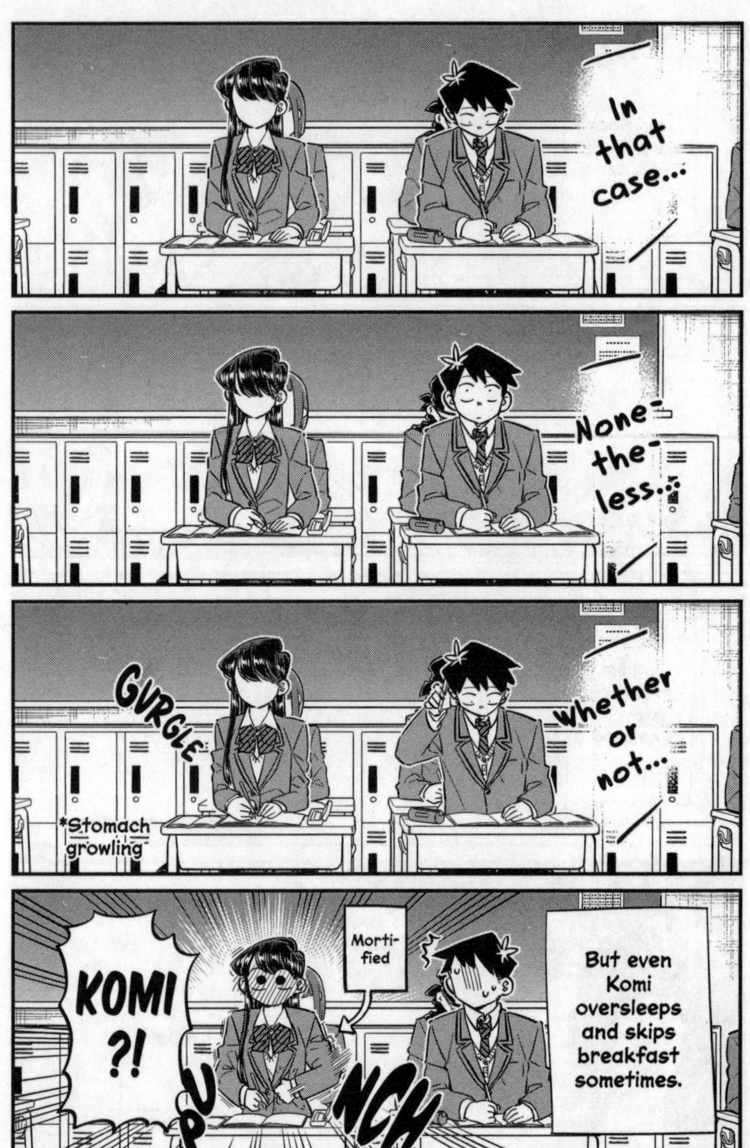
In that case...
None-the-less...
GURGLE
*Stomach growling
whether or not...
KOMI ?!
Morti-fied
But even Komi oversleeps and skips breakfast sometimes.
UP
NCH

Communication 80: Invitation to Lunch

MY NAME IS MAKOTO KATAI.

MY HOBBY IS PATCH-WORK QUILTING.
SNIIRK

THE OTHER DAY, I MADE MY FIRST FRIEND (TADANO) ...
...AND GAINED A MASTER IN THE ART OF COMMUNICATION (KOMI).
MY HIGH SCHOOL LIFE IS TAKING OFF!!

TODAY, I'M GOING TO INVITE TADANO TO LUNCH!
WATCH THIS, MASTER !!
SNIIRK
SHIVER
Feeling a chill

ALL RIGHT ...
... HERE GOES.
FWOOO
BABMP BABMP
I PRACTICED EXACTLY WHAT TO SAY!

T-TADANO.
RRR RMMMMMMMMN
GAH! THAT SOUNDED GRUFF!!
AND OVERLY FAMILIAR!!
JOLT
... SIR?
Y-YES, KATAI?

...
...

I FORGOT WHAT I WAS GONNA SAY!!
?!

AND KOMI IS WATCHING!
SH-SHE'S SO INTIMIDATING!
STARE
HUFF
HUFF
STARE

HEY, UM...
DOES HE WANT TO HAVE LUNCH TOGETHER?
...

"LET'S EAT OUT-SIDE! ♪" WAS THAT IT?
NO, IT'S COLD OUTSIDE ...
BUT PEOPLE WILL SEE US IN HERE, SO...
COME ON! SAY SOME-THING!
BUT WHAT IF I JUST ANNOY HIM?!
AND HE MIGHT THINK I DON'T HAVE OTHER FRIENDS!
SMILE! SMILE!
JUST SAY SOME-THING INVITING!

Let's take this out-side.
SMIIIRK
?!
How every-one (even Katai) feels

MURMUR
MURMUR
I DID IT AGAIN...
I'M SO RUDE...
STRIIIDE
I WISH I COULD CRAWL INTO A HOLE!

SORRY, BUT I SHOULD GO WITH HIM.
?!
He's going?!

WHY DO I ALWAYS DO THIS?
SOB
HEEEY
!

HEY! KATAI!
IT'S A MIRA-CLE!!

Lunch

AWESOME! LUNCH WITH A PAL!
AHHHHH
IT'S A DREAM COME TRUE!!

I BET MASTER PUT IN A GOOD WORD FOR ME!
Go on!
*Only in his imagination
THANK YOU, COMMUNICATION MASTER!
HM?

MASTER ?!
WHY DID YOU COME TOO?!
Was worried about Tadano

OH, RIGHT ...
EATING TO-GETHER ISN'T MY ONLY GOAL!
WE NEED TO HAVE FUN AND BOND!!
YAAAY
GOAL

MASTER IS WATCHING OVER ME!
BUT SHE DOESN'T HAVE TO!
BE-CAUSE I GOT THIS!

...
Let's eat!
Hey, Katai.
Your lunch looks good.
Did your mother make it?

WHAT DO YOU DO FOR FUN?
IS THIS A FIRST DATE ?!

UM, I LIKE MOVIES AND VIDEO GAMES.
OH.
...
...

YES! DIDN'T THAT CON-VERSATION GO WELL, MASTER ?!
GLOWER
SHE DOESN'T LOOK IM-PRESSED !!
Komi can't compre-hend what she's seeing.

I NEED TO SHOW HER TADANO AND I ARE TIGHT!
AND I KNOW EXACTLY HOW!

HERE. SAY, "AH."
Even Tadano was taken aback.

But he ate it anyway.
CHOMP
?!

YEAH!! HOW WAS THAT, MASTER?! TADANO AND I–
GLOWER
IT WASN'T ENOUGH ?! YOU'RE SO STRICT!!
Komi is experi-encing complicated feelings.

BUT WHAT ELSE CAN I DO?
AHA!!

M-MASTER ALREADY SHOWED ME THE WAY!!
IT'S A L-LITTLE EMBAR-RASSING, BUT I'LL DO IT!!

SWUP
FUMP

GLOMP
??!!

CHAPTER 1, PAGE 12 OF 51 HOSTESS TIPS ☆ FOR GETTING CLOSE ♡ ENCOURAGES PHYSICAL CONTACT!!
MASTER WAS TELLING ME TO DO THIS!
Like this
IT'S EMBAR-RASSING, BUT IF IT WORKS ...
GLANCE

...!
HE SEEMS UNCOM-FORTABLE !!

GLOMMMP
UM...
HUH? HE SEEMS ...
UH...
OH MAN...
NOW WHAT SHOULD I DO?!
Still clinging to him

From Komi's viewpoint
YOU ATE MY LUNCH, MAN!
NOW YOU GOTTA PAY UP!
The shakedown
?!

Wants to intervene but can't
?!
?!
!!
IT LOOKS LIKE MASTER WANTS TO COME TO MY AID!
HURRY, MASTER!! I CAN'T DO THIS!!
Chaos

YOU DON'T ...
...HAVE TO TRY SO HARD.
HUH?
I DON'T COMPLETELY UNDER-STAND, BUT...

...YOU CAN ACT NORMAL AROUND ME.

THAT'S ENOUGH FOR ME.

...!

OKAY.

!!
IS THAT KOMI?
GROWWWL
#Stomach growling
BLUSHHHH
KOMI, WOULD YOU LIKE TO JOIN US?
I'LL INTRO-DUCE YOU TO KATAI!
Eat lunch?! With Master?!
...
SWIP
...

...

NOD

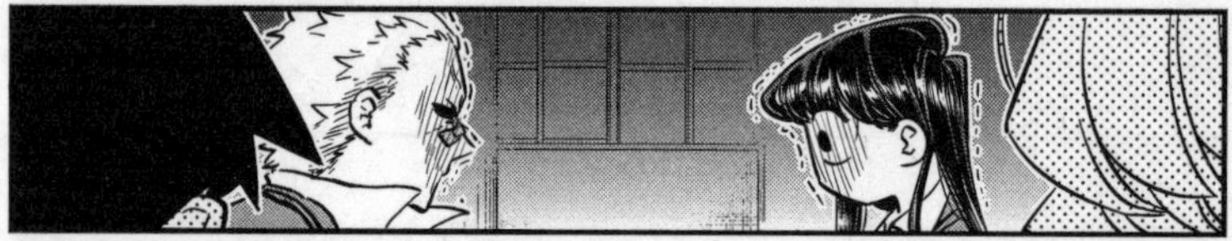

Communication 80 — The End

Komi Can't Communicate

Komi Can't Communicate

Communication 81: Cat Cafe

I saw it on the news.
OH, A CAT CAFE?!

Wants to invite them to go
TREMMMBLE

HMPH
Cat Komi hasn't been around for a while...
She's working up her courage.

Shall we go together?
HARD NOPE!
THAT WAS BLUNT!!
SHOCK

OH, RIGHT. NAJIMI IS ALLERGIC TO CATS.
!
Yeah... I'd wuv to kiss da wittle kitties, but... ❤
FIDGET FIDGET
You're creepy.

...

Won-dering about Tadano
GLANCE
HM?
ME?

...
?

UM, I'M BUSY TODAY, SO...
... HOW ABOUT INVITING SOMEONE ELSE? LIKE ONEMINE!
!

MAYBE THAT'S HARD FOR HER TO DO...
...
MEOW WA HA

Has difficulty inviting people besides Tadano and Naji–
YOU RANG?
SHE JUST SHOWED UP?!

Try inviting her!
!

Cat power
SURE, I'LL GO!
ONEMINE'S SO DEPENDABLE!

CAT CAFE GATEAU
Cat Cafe Gateau

TA DA! I CAME TOOOOOO!
TA DA AA
YEAH. YOU CAME WITH ME. SO I KNOW THAT.

Recep-tion
MEEEEOW
RUB
!

!! !! !! !! !! !! !! !! !! !! !! !! !! !!
?!
?!!
Komi is shocked by how cute they are.

Hm? What the?
!!
!!

RUB RUB
!

JOLT
HUFF
HUFF
HUFF
?!

TREMMMBLE
?!

IT LOOKS LIKE THE CATS JUST RUN FREE.

AND THEY *LOVE* PEOPLE!
RUB RUB
MEOW
THEY'RE VERY FRIENDLY! MEOW!

SILENCE
No cats are visiting Komi.
HM?

TREMBLE
K...
KAEDE, HOW ARE *YOU* DOING?

THERE, THERE... GOOOOOOD KITTY...
SWARM
SWARM
CATS EVERY-WHERE !!

PF FFF FBB BBB TTT TT!
K-KAEDE ?
KAEDE ?!

HUFF
HUFF
HUFF
Insanely jealous
I'VE NEVER SEEN A FACE LIKE THAT BEFORE!!

ZZZ
LOOK, KOMI!
THERE'S ONE NAPPING UP THERE. TRY PETTING IT!
ZZZ
IF IT'S ASLEEP, IT CAN'T RUN AWAY...
!
HUFF
HUFF

WANDER
WANDER
WANDER
WANDER

Doesn't want to wake it
SHE EVEN HAS A COMMUNICATION DISORDER WITH CATS?!

MY NAME IS CHOCOLAT (♀).
AND I'M THE BOSS OF THIS CAT CAFE.

AS USUAL, THE STUPID HUMANS ARE HANGING AROUND.

I HATE IT WHEN THEY TOUCH ME.
THEY ALWAYS TOUCH US WITHOUT A CARE FOR HOW WE FEEL!
LIKE WHEN I'VE JUST SMOOTHED MY FUR AND—
BOSS! BOSS!
DERE'S A SCARY HUMAN HERE!

DON'T INTER-RUPT ME!!
CHOCOLAT Cat punch!
GYAAAAH!

ANYWAY, WHAT DID YOU SAY?
DERE'S A SCARY HUMAN!
I DUNNO WHAT SHE'S THINKIN'!
SHE'S GOT A SPWOOKY AURA!

AN AURA, YOU SAY?
Cat-nip chew toy
WHICH GIRL?
UM...

...D-DAT ONE!
DA FEMALE WIT' DA BLACK FUR!
HUNH? THAT'S JUST A NORMAL–

FWIP
Black cat!!
*Likes black cats
JOLT
?!

YEAH, SHE'S KIND OF MYSTE-RIOUS.
SNIF SNIF

I'LL KEEP AN EYE ON HER ...

SCATTER
WHAT'S GOING ON? SHE ISN'T INTERACTING WITH US AT ALL!

BUT IT SEEMS LIKE SHE WANTS TO...
HA HA! SERVES YOU RIGHT!

BWA HA HA...
...

TCH... WHAT A PITIFUL HUMAN!
HMFPH
WHAH? BOSS?
ROLL ROLL
WHERE YA GOIN'?

Boss!!
THOMP
Boss?!

Boss?
Seriously, Boss?
You visitin' dat female?
whoa...

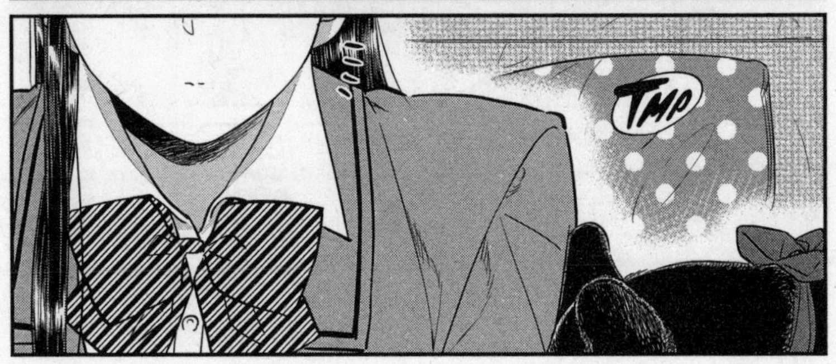
TMP
...

MEOW!

!

MEOW!

Tadano didn't have plans. He only declined because he wanted Komi to practice asking other people.
Mistake!
He agonized over whether to use that photo for his cell phone wallpaper for three days.
I SHOULD'VE GONE!!

Communication 81 — The End

Komi Can't Communicate

Communication 82: Final Exam

...
Komi only has two pencils.

...!
Has to tell the teacher

...

...!!
But she's too embar-rassed.

KOMI ISN'T WRITING ANY-THING.

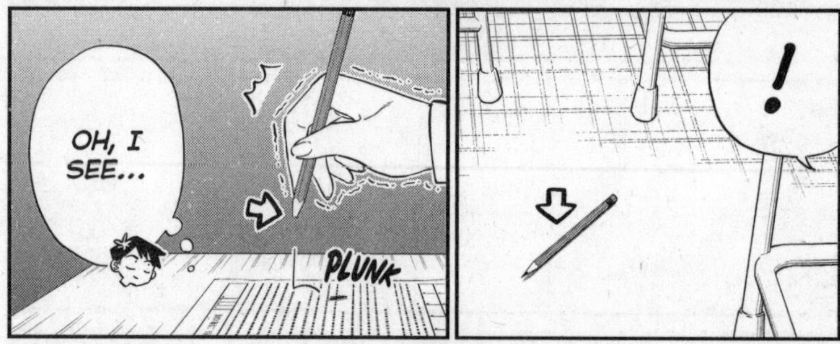
!
OH, I SEE...
PLUNK

...
I THINK IT'S AROUND HERE ...
ROLLL

EXCUSE ME! I DROPPED MY PENCIL!
HUUUUUH?
Would you please pick it up?

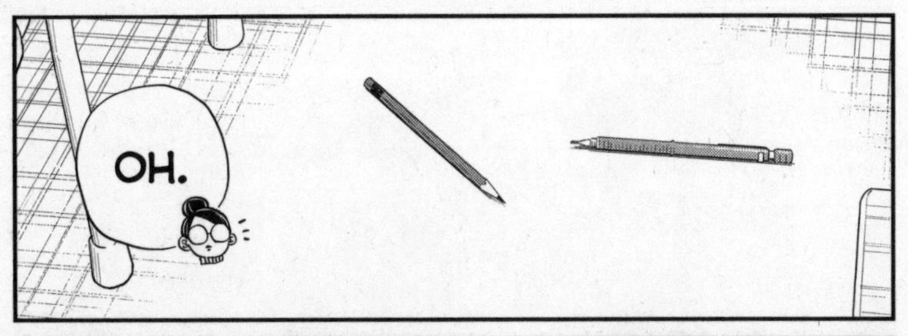
OH.

IS THIS KOMI'S?
HERE.
SHE'S THE ONLY ONE WHO USES A WOODEN PENCIL.

PROB-LEM SOLVED!
HA HA... KOMI CAN BE SO CARE-LESS!
HEY...
HM?
WHERE'S MY ERASER?

I DIDN'T GET IT OUT!!
That was *care-less.*

...
I'll try not to make any—
Oops!
SKRK SKRK SKRK SKR-
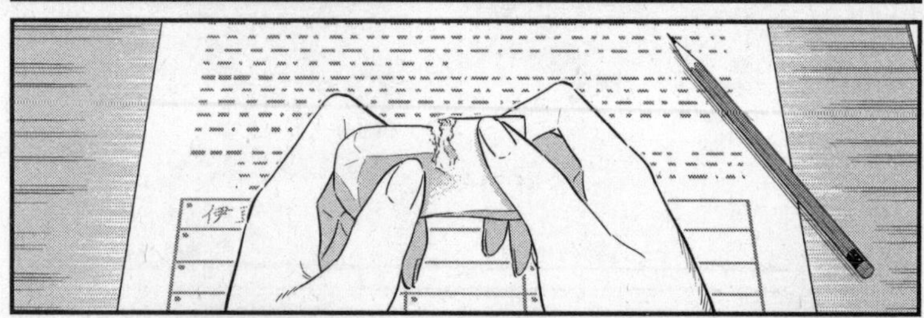

PLONK
!

HM?

Communication 82 — The End

Hitohito! Lend me an eraser!
Sis

HE TREASURED IT

Never.
T

Komi Can't Communicate

Communication 83: The Love Game

WEL-
COME
TO THE
LOVE
GAME!!
THE PLAYERS HAVE TO SAY "I LOVE YOU" TO SOMEONE. AND IF THEY LAUGH OR BLUSH, THEY LOSE!
IT'S OKAY TO BE CREATIVE IN CHANGING THE WORDING OR GENERATING A MOOD!

BUT IF YOU CRACK UP, YOU LOSE!!
I LOVE YOU.
SMIIIRK
LOSER!
*Demonstration by Tadano and Katai

YAMAI REALLY WANTED TO PLAY THIS WITH KOMI!!
KOMI'S GOOD AT THIS!

I JUST WANT TO TELL KOMI I LOVE HER!! WHO CARES ABOUT WINNING?!
I JUST WANT TO DECLARE MY LOVE !!!
...

IT'S YOUR TURN, KOMI!
SO SAY IT TO ME!
!

HERE IT COMES!!! WHAT I'VE BEEN WAITING FOR!! AND THROUGH LEGAL MEANS !!
THIS IS IT!!!

I WONDER HOW SHE'LL SAY IT! HM? HUH? YEAH? COME ON! SAY IT!! "I..." "I LOVE..." "I LOVE YOU!"

SNICKER
She cracked before Komi did anything.

LET'S DO IT AGAIN!
What's up? Whatcha doin'?
URGH! NAJIMI'S INTER-RUPTING!

HM? HMM? WE'RE NOT DOING ANY-THING!
RIGHT, KOMI?
?!
Huh? Really?
REALLY! SOLO HIDE-AND-SEEK IS A HUNDRED TIMES MORE FUN!
So go play it!
HA HA HA HA HA HA HA HA HA HA HA HA HA HA

BY THE WAY, KOMI...

...I'm in love with you!!
ARGH!!
SPLURT

Huh? Komi cracked up!!
I win !!
SHAKE SHAKE
Tadano! You be the judge!!
HUH? ME?

Only snorted in surprise

KOMI DIDN'T BLUSH, SO SHE WON.
That's favor-itism!
Starting to enjoy the game

TEE HEE HEE!
FWIP
I! LUV! YOUUU!

...

BAM
...
I LOVE YOU.

...
KOMI'S UNBEAT-ABLE!!

IT'S TIME TO DEPLOY OUR BIG GUNS!
Tada-no! Come on!
HUH?! ME?!
?!

...
I...

I C-C-C-C-C-AN'T D-D-D-D-DO IT!
TREMBLE
N-
NOD NOD
WHAT WAS THAT PAUSE FOR?!

WHY SO EMBAR-RASSED? IT'S JUST A GAME!
IF YOU RESIST ...
Tadano, you know what'll happen!
...IT'LL MAKE IT SEEM LIKE THERE'S A REASON FOR THAT!
URGH !!

TH-THERE'S NO ESCAPE!
URGH... THAT ONION-HEAD IS SO SLY WITH WORDS!
Hurry! Do it!
Onion-head

IT...IT'S JUST A GAME!!
I DON'T NEED TO BE EMBARRASSED! I CAN PLAY IT LIKE A JOKE!
S-so here goes...

...
...

I...
HEH
And yer out!!

WHAT?! THE SPEAKER CAN'T LAUGH EITHER?!
OF COURSE NOT! IT'S EMBARRASSING FOR BOTH SIDES!
It's that kind of game!
OH... RIGHT, RIGHT!

The love game is over.
I heard wombats have square poop!
I can't use that tomorrow!

K-KOMI SEEMED COMPLETELY CALM.
BUT SHE WOULDN'T CARE IF I SAID I LOVED HER! HA HA HA...
Ah ha ha!
I'M OVERTHINKING IT!!

Going to the ladies' room?
See ya later!!
I'll go too!
SWIP

Komi was relieved that Najimi stopped Tadano and dis-appointed that he didn't say it.
BONK

Communication 83 — The End

Communication 84: Roasted Potatoes

GLANCE
GLANCE
Roasted potatoes...
!
GWOOO
?!

Ghost
Uneasy about speaking to him
PHEW

ROASTED POTATOES
?
!
JOLT

SH-SHAKE SHAKE
Finally managed to shake her head

Roasted pota-toes ...
?!
?!
Doesn't know why she shook her head

!
!

...

!!
!!

Cowering
...

!
ROASTED POTATOES
300
ser-vice
BWOOOOOO

ONE...

TWO

FIVE!!

Komi successfully made the purchase.
Thank ya!

♪
♪...
♪
Worried five may be too many

!
HWOO

WARM
WARM WARM
WARM

Communication 84 — The End

Communication 85: Memories of the Culture Festival

UAAARGH! WHY DID I DO THAT?!
I SHOULD'VE AT LEAST CHANGED FOR THE DANCE!!
TOSS
GYA-AAH!
GYAA-AHHH!!
TURN
Tadano's dark history gained a new page.

AM I JUST A DUMB STUDENT WHO GETS CARRIED AWAY?!
Yes, he is.
GRR
GRRR! HOW CAN I RELIEVE MY FRUS-TRATION?!
GRR
GRR

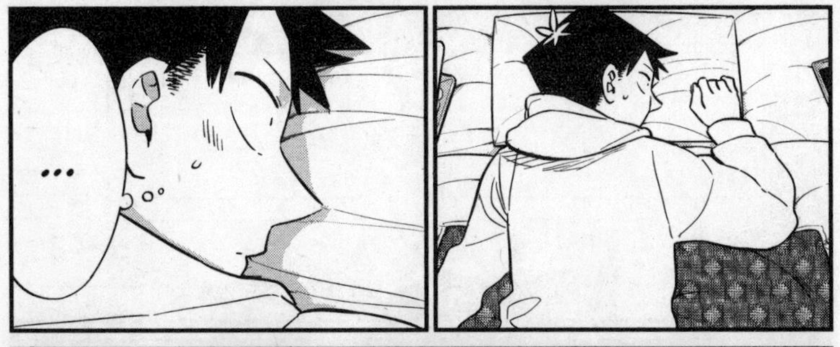
...

KOMI'S FACE THAT NIGHT...

THIS IS...
WHAT WAS I STARTING TO SAY?

NO, NO, NO, NO, NO, NO, NO WAY!!!
SHAKE SHAKE SHAKE SHAKE SHAKE SHAKE SHAKE SHAKE
WHAT'RE YOU DOING?! DON'T SHAKE THE BED!

THINK ABOUT IT.
SHWUF
YOU WOULD NEVER FEEL THAT WAY.

I MEAN, KOMI'S PRETTY ...
...AND SHE'S CUTE...
...BUT HER AND ME?

NO, NO, NO, NO, NO! DON'T THINK THAT!!
I'M GOING OUT FOR A BIT.

TO BUY SOME-THING?
Like girlie mags?
N-NO!

WHAT TIMING !!

G-GOOD EVENING, KOMI!
W- WHAT A COINCI- DENCE!
!!

!!

?
YOU BOUGHT ROASTED POTA- TOES?
BLUSH
N-NOD

IT'S LATE, SO I'LL SEE YOU HOME.
?
SHAKE SHAKE

OH... YOU'RE ALL RIGHT?
N-
NOD NOD

...
...

SHOULD I ASK HER TO HANG OUT?
IT'S WINTER VACA-TION...
...
...WHEN I'M WITH HER...
...IT'S FUN, SO...
...AND, UM...

BUT ONLY AS FRIENDS!
KLUNK
AS FRIENDS! YEAH!
?

BUT IF I'M GOING TO INVITE HER SOME-WHERE...
...I NEED TO HAVE A DATE ...
...AND A SPECIFIC ACTIVITY.

...
...

SWOOO
WELL, TAKE CARE!
I MISSED MY CHANCE !!

TUG
!

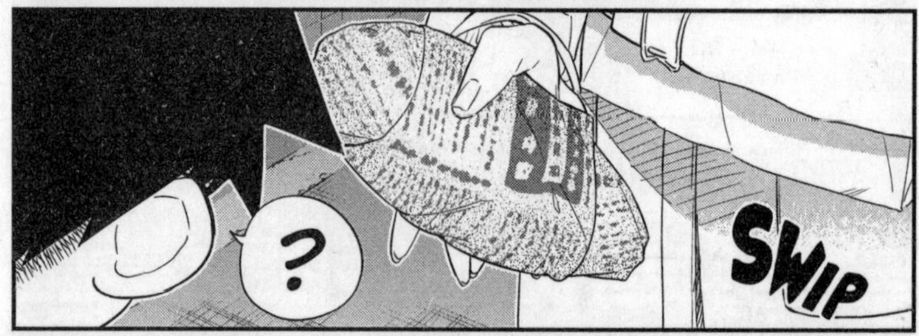
SWIP
?

OH, YOU'RE GIVING ME ONE?
THANK YOU!

WARM

LET'S HANG OUT SOME-TIME...

...DURING WINTER BREAK!

Communication 85 — The End

Komi Can't Communicate

Komi Can't Communicate Bonus

Can Komi Make 100 Friends?: The Steep Path

Komi Can't Communicate Bonus

Can Komi Make 100 Friends?: Kitty Paradise

JING
JANG
Welcome!
Cat Cafe Gateau
PWAH
!
Chocolat put a paw print in Komi's Book of Friends.
Only 85 to go!! Meow!

Komi Can't Communicate

VOL. 6
Shonen Sunday Edition

Story and Art by Tomohito Oda

English Translation & Adaptation/John Werry
Touch-Up Art & Lettering/Eve Grandt
Design/Julian [JR] Robinson
Editor/Pancha Diaz

COMI-SAN WA, COMYUSHO DESU. Vol. 6
by Tomohito ODA

Original Japanese edition published by SHOGAKUKAN.
English translation rights in the United States of America, Canada, the United Kingdom, Ireland, Australia and New Zealand arranged with SHOGAKUKAN.

Original Cover Design/Masato ISHIZAWA + Bay Bridge Studio

Printed in the U.S.A.

Published by VIZ Media, LLC
P.O. Box 77010
San Francisco, CA 94107

10 9 8 7 6 5 4 3 2 1
First printing, April 2020

viz.com

shonensunday.com

PARENTAL ADVISORY
KOMI CAN'T COMMUNICATE is rated T for Teen and is recommended for ages 13 and up.

Tomohito Oda won the grand prize for *World Worst One* in the 70th Shogakukan New Comic Artist Awards in 2012. Oda's series *Digicon*, about a tough high school girl who finds herself in control of an alien with plans for world domination, ran from 2014 to 2015. In 2015, *Komi Can't Communicate* debuted as a one-shot in *Weekly Shonen Sunday* and was picked up as a full series by the same magazine in 2016.

This is the last page!

Komi Can't Communicate has been printed in the original Japanese format to preserve the orientation of the artwork.

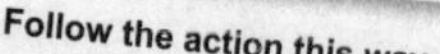

Follow the action this way.